Step into the Desert

Howard Rice

Consultant

Timothy Rasinski, Ph.D.
Kent State University

Publishing Credits

Dona Herweck Rice, *Editor-in-Chief*
Robin Erickson, *Production Director*
Lee Aucoin, *Creative Director*
Conni Medina, M.A.Ed., *Editorial Director*
Jamey Acosta, *Editor*
Stephanie Reid, *Photo Editor*
Rachelle Cracchiolo, M.S.Ed., *Publisher*

Based on writing from *TIME For Kids*.

TIME For Kids and the *TIME For Kids* logo are registered trademarks of TIME Inc. Used under license.

Teacher Created Materials

5301 Oceanus Drive
Huntington Beach, CA 92649-1030
http://www.tcmpub.com

ISBN 978-1-4333-3629-4

© 2012 Teacher Created Materials, Inc.
Reprinted 2013

Table of Contents

Where Are You?

Look around. The sky is big and blue. The ground is dry and bare. Hills of sand cross the land as far as you can see. In the distance, a string of camels walks slowly in the rising sun. It is hot and getting hotter.

Where are you?
You are in a **desert**, of course!

What Is a Desert?

A desert is an area of land with very little rain and, most of the time, high temperatures during the day.

In a desert, there is less than 10 inches of rain each year. The ground is usually dry.

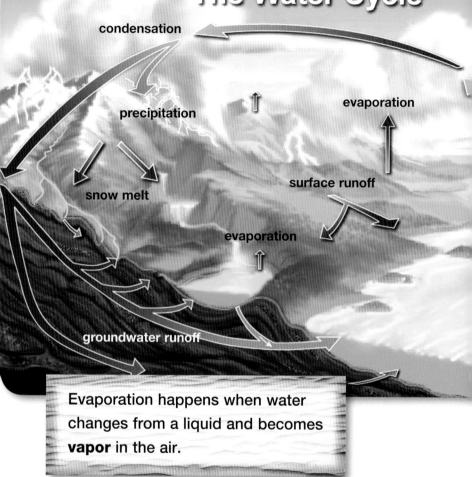

The Water Cycle

condensation

precipitation

evaporation

snow melt

surface runoff

evaporation

groundwater runoff

Evaporation happens when water changes from a liquid and becomes **vapor** in the air.

Whenever it rains in a desert, the heat of the sun dries up most of the water. This is called **evaporation** (ih-vap-uh-REY-shuhn).

condensation

evaporation

One reason for evaporation is the high temperatures. Desert nights can be cold because during the night the ground releases its heat. But during the day, the ground soaks up the heat.

The temperature in the desert can reach as high as 130°F!

How hot is that? Most people
are comfortable at about 70°F.
Deserts can get almost twice that hot!

Where Are They?

Most of the deserts are in two areas called the *Tropic of Cancer* and the *Tropic of Capricorn*. Look at the map to find the tropics. The map also shows where you can find the world's great deserts.

Tropic of Cancer

Equator

Tropic of Capricorn

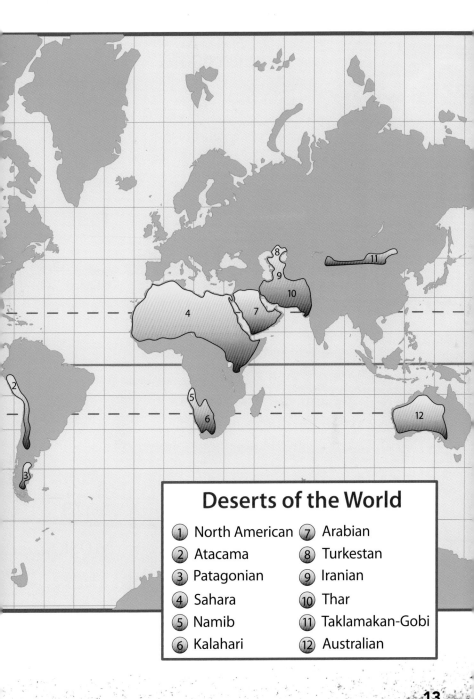

Deserts of the World

1. North American
2. Atacama
3. Patagonian
4. Sahara
5. Namib
6. Kalahari
7. Arabian
8. Turkestan
9. Iranian
10. Thar
11. Taklamakan-Gobi
12. Australian

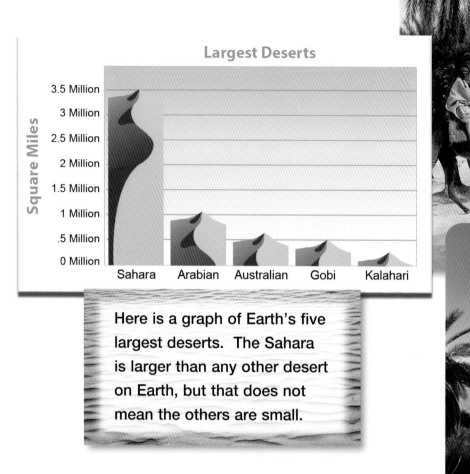

Largest Deserts

Square Miles

| | 3.5 Million | 3 Million | 2.5 Million | 2 Million | 1.5 Million | 1 Million | .5 Million | 0 Million |

Sahara   Arabian   Australian   Gobi   Kalahari

Here is a graph of Earth's five largest deserts. The Sahara is larger than any other desert on Earth, but that does not mean the others are small.

The largest desert in the world is the **Sahara**. It is in Africa. Most of the Sahara gets no rain, but there are many underground rivers. Water sometimes rises to the land.

Desert heat sometimes makes people think they see an oasis that is not really there.

Then an **oasis** (oh-EY-sis) is formed. An oasis is a wet and green area in the middle of a desert.

How Are They Formed?

Many deserts are formed because of mountains. High mountains keep **moisture** (MOIS-cher) from getting past them.

Rain and snow fall on the mountains, but the air is dry by the time it gets to the desert.

Some deserts are formed because the land is too far away from bodies of water. The air soaks up water from lakes and oceans. Then it rains. But the rain cannot make it all the way to the desert.

Even though there is not much of it, water changes the shape of deserts. So does wind.

You can try an erosion experiment. Make a small hill out of sand. Pour water from a pitcher down the side of the hill. What happens? Erosion!

Water and wind cause desert **erosion** (ih-ROH-zhuhn). Since the land is so dry, it wears away when water or wind comes. That is what erosion means.

Strong desert winds blast and change rocks. Wind also moves sand and forms **dunes** (DOONZ). Dunes are like little hills spread across the desert.

When the wind comes from one direction, the dune is shaped like a moon. When the wind comes from many directions, the dune looks more like a star.

Can Anything Live There?

cactus flower

dung beetle

scorpion

Even though there is little
water, many deserts have plant and
animal life.

Joshua tree

The seeds of some desert plants may wait a long time underground. Once there is rain, they grow and bloom quickly. Other plants have long, deep roots that reach far below the ground for water.

roadrunner

bearded lizard

yucca

Animals in the desert have found ways to live with little water. Some sleep during the dry season. Some are able to live without water for a long time. Many sleep during the day and come out at night when it is cooler. Some even reuse the water that is already inside of them!

kangaroo rat

coyote

Desert life is not for everyone. The heat and lack of water make it difficult. But as these plants and animals show, it can be done!

Glossary

desert—an area of land with very little rain and usually high temperatures

dunes—the hills of sand formed by wind

erosion—the wearing away of land caused by water, wind, or ice

evaporation—the changing of water from liquid into vapor

moisture—a small amount of liquid, usually water

oasis—an area of land in a desert with water and growing plants

Sahara—the largest desert in the world

vapor—the gas form of a liquid